THE
TEAMBUILDING
POCKETBOOK

By Paul Tizzard

Drawings by Phil Hailstone

"A fantastic little book filled with fun, innovative and practical activities that engage teams at whatever stage of their development. Simply a 'must have' for anyone involved with or dealing with teams."

Claire Paul, Learning & Development Consultant, City & Guilds

"This practical collection of creative activities is a must for managers, consultants and trainers who want quick and easy exercises that will get results. One to have within easy reach, as you'll use it regularly!"

Vicky Harris, Learning & Development Consultant, Virgin Atlantic Airways

Published by:
Management Pocketbooks Ltd
Laurel House, Station Approach,
Alresford, Hants SO24 9JH, U.K.
Tel: +44 (0)1962 735573
Fax: +44 (0)1962 733637
E-mail: sales@pocketbook.co.uk
Website: www.pocketbook.co.uk

This edition published 2006. Reprinted 2007.

© Paul Tizzard 2006.

British Library Cataloguing-in-Publication Data – A
catalogue record for this book is available from the
British Library.

ISBN-13   978 1 903776 42 1

Design, typesetting and graphics by **efex ltd**.
Printed in U.K.

Acknowledgements and thanks

I would like to thank the following who have taught
me so much about teams and team dynamics:

Andy Cross for his contributions and for providing a
proper coaching role model by proving that you can
coach no matter how high up you are in the
organisation's food chain.

Julia Philpott and Richard Conway for being the
opposite type to me on most profiles and showing
the value of having a balanced team with
complementary roles.

Barrie Watson of Belbin Associates for emphasizing
the importance of playing to your strengths.

Team Management Systems Development
International, York for teaching me about the power
of building a balanced team.

Insights International, Dundee for teaching me how
to engage small to large groups in psychometrics
and for helping me to understand Jung.

Alan Evans for his help and nice comments
about the book.

CONTENTS

FOREWORD BY DR. MEREDITH BELBIN

Paul Tizzard has compiled an amazing range of quick, easily digestible exercises suitable for any group of people wishing to improve their teamwork and restricted by having only limited time available. Most of the exercises take a mere 10 minutes. Some are shorter still. None last longer than 30 minutes. This compilation of miscellaneous activities is notable also in reflecting no one school of thought. The reader is free to choose that which appeals.

The Teambuilding Pocketbook can, if one chooses, be treated like a lucky dip offering valued surprises even for less diligent readers. But those who have the patience to read the Pocketbook throughout will find it even more worthwhile.

Meredith Belbin

January 2006

1INTRODUCTION

INTRODUCTION

WORKING IN TEAMS

It is almost certain in today's workplace that at some point you will find yourself in a team, whether you like it or not. The saying that *you pick your friends not your family*, can, with a little adaptation, be just as true for a lot of teams. Ideally, your team will be made up of an even mix of types, carefully selected to ensure there are no gaps in terms of the roles people need to perform. But in reality this is rarely how teams are formed.

Sometimes a group of people work together, even share meetings and team time of some description but cannot be described as a genuine team. If you manage this kind of group and want to turn them into a more coherent team, use some of the activities in this book to help achieve this. If you are a training consultant being asked to intervene in a team's development, you naturally want to make the right intervention as you are going to have an impact.

WORKING IN TEAMS

This book is for managers, team leaders and trainers and is full of practical activities and ideas to help you make your team time as effective and as pleasant as it can be. There are ideas for managers and leaders to use during team meetings and briefings, and ideas for trainers running a team build.

I have been working with teams for many years. I have training and experience in nearly all the major team psychometrics and have drawn on this in compiling these activities. The book is divided into snappy sections to make it easy to access what you need. Simply find the section that applies to your team and within it will be some ideas that you can use straight away.

These activities are based on real situations. Anyone who works in a team knows what it feels like when people are arguing, or when meetings are a waste of time. This book will help you get the teams you work with into a more productive state.

TEAM PURPOSE

If you do only one thing for your team, help them to understand the purpose of their work, their role, their team and, in turn, the organisation.

In Victor Frankl's book *Man's Search for Meaning* he wrote about his time in the concentration camps. He claimed that the reason for his survival was that he found a purpose to live for. He imagined leaving the camp and then writing books and talking about the whole experience so that it would never ever be repeated. This image was so powerful that it was the reason, he claimed, that he stayed alive.

Think about a time when you have worked on something and started to doubt whether it was actually worth it, or if the effort was going to be rewarded (or even noticed). How motivated did you feel about the work? Part of the essential role of team leaders and consultants, when working with or in teams, is **to help people to find meaning in what they do**.

INTRODUCTION

TEAMBUILDING

At least once a month I get asked: '**Can I have a team build please?**' But the training consultants and managers who ask me use these words to cover a wide range of situations within teams. The team may be in the early stages of forming, they may be arguing constantly or they may need remotivating. You need quite different activities for each stage of a team's development, so it is important to **know your starting point** before you decide what is required.

Of course, you don't know what is really going on in a team unless you are in it. (Sometimes not even then!) But, as a manager or training consultant, whatever you do with a team will have an effect. Just going to talk to the team will have an effect.

As a minimum, approach any team event you organise as an opportunity for the group to come together and have something worthwhile to talk about afterwards. Even the annual Christmas party provides a (hopefully positive) shared experience, creating a familiar glow that can last for weeks afterwards. What sort of team atmosphere and conversation do you want to generate after your team event?

WAYS OF WORKING

The following terms describe some of the interactions within teams:

Teamworking – a group of people, normally but not always geographically close to each other, interact on certain work matters. They have regular meetings and are perhaps involved with joint problem solving, but the work does not require them to know each other really well. (For great ideas in this area, see *The Teamworking Pocketbook* by Ian Fleming.)

Teambuilding – a group of people are brought together who need to work at a more intimate level of understanding. They may have reached this stage over a period of time, but it is more likely that the manager is actively working to form them into a certain kind of team. This book is firmly about teambuilding.

Team development – work that helps teams to become high-performing. Most of the activities contained within the PAUL model in this book fit into the category of team development as you work towards building the team.

Team time – a general term that I use to label what really happens when people come together! What are the stories that are told within and about the team? What is the climate of the team? What is the energy like? Are people's efforts all pointing in the same direction?

TEAMWORKING

This book is about teambuilding. If **teamworking** relates to a team's arrangements and organisational issues then teambuilding is about developing its culture and relationships.

Teamworking is the tip of the iceberg. It is visible and tangible and deals with practicalities. Some examples:

- How desks are positioned in relation to each other
- How many meetings the team holds
- Where appraisals are held
- Who works with whom on what bits of work
- Who leads the meetings
- Who chairs the meetings and who types up the minutes

Teamworking addresses the behaviour level: things that are easier to see.

TEAMBUILDING

Teambuilding is what is below the iceberg's tip. It is sometimes unseen but is definitely felt and mostly known. It is, for example:

- The look between two team members when a third person talks

- The silent resentments felt when one person is allocated a particular piece of work that someone else wanted

- What really happens after people leave the meetings

- The stories that the team tells about itself and the leader

- The identity the team has to the outside organisation or customer

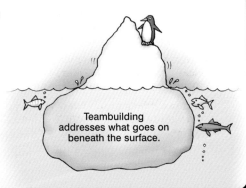

Teambuilding addresses what goes on beneath the surface.

INTRODUCTION

TEAMWORKING VS TEAMBUILDING

In summary, if you want to work on organising your team, or communicating better over specific pieces of work, these are **teamworking** issues and need activities that focus on particular problem areas. (An example that I use for teams who need help with communication is: 'The Silurians are coming to town' by Mike Fenwick in *Team Challenges*, published by Fenman. This activity withholds key bits of information from the players so that they are forced to talk to each other more about what they know. It encourages people to ask questions, listen to each other and work collaboratively.)

Activities suitable for teamworking address issues at a skills level and do not really venture into such scary areas as, *'Why is it that Ajay does not talk to Sarah during our team meetings – what is really going on?'*

In a **teambuilding** approach, we go deeper. We examine the slightly uncomfortable areas that people find it hard to talk about, such as: *'These are my goals in this company…'*.

(13)

TEAM STAGES
WHERE ARE YOU NOW?

The first step towards undertaking some teambuilding is to identify the stage of development your team has currently reached.

I have put together a model, loosely based on Tuckman's four stages of team development, to help you identify what is happening in the team you need to work with.

Caution
Teams are full of erratic human beings who are not very easy to measure. They will not necessarily fall into neat groups like those in the PAUL model below!

TEAM STAGES

WHERE ARE YOU NOW?

Read the description of the four stages in the **PAUL** model and tick any relevant boxes to give you some idea of your team's current stage.

Polite stage
- ❑ Awkwardness
- ❑ Extremely polite
- ❑ Some people not talking at all (appear to be holding back)
- ❑ Getting to know each other

Angry stage (plus many other emotions)
- ❑ Role manoeuvring
- ❑ People starting to assert themselves
- ❑ Some jostling for position
- ❑ Emotion expressed in passive-aggressive manner

TEAM STAGES
WHERE ARE YOU NOW?

Please tick any relevant boxes to give you some idea of your team's current stage.

Understanding stage
- ❑ Plateau
- ❑ Drifting
- ❑ No direction
- ❑ Comfortable

Learning stage
- ❑ Self-directed
- ❑ Highly motivated
- ❑ Self-coaching
- ❑ Performing at high levels

GROUPS VS TEAMS

High performing teams (the table below* is based on Dr. Meredith Belbin's research) are not the norm. The majority of us probably belong to looser teams, more like his description of a group. Try using the factors in the table as headings to check your team's current position and consider how you can move closer to the right hand column.

Factor	Group or 'team'	High performing team
Size	Unlimited	Limited (normally 6-8)
Leadership style	Dictatorial or non-existent	Mixture of authoritative and coaching style**
Different viewpoints	Unwelcome	Welcome
Goals	May or may not have goals	Agreed and shared goals
Recruitment of members	You arrived and they were already there!	You considered gaps in the team and recruited for them
Membership	Conformance	Complementary roles
Decision-making	Top down	Shared
Review	Self-reflection on personal agenda	Shared feedback on team effectiveness
Problems	Blame culture	Mutual support
Relationships	Adversaries	Friends

*Adapted and reproduced with kind permission of Barrie Watson, Cert Consultancy – providers of accredited Belbin training

** See further Harvard Business Review, March 2000. Article by Daniel Goleman, 'Leadership that gets results'.

INTRODUCTION

TEAM SELF-ASSESSMENT

If you are in a regular 'we sit near each other' sort of team, please don't despair. The criteria on the previous page are more likely to belong to a team selected with a specific end point in mind. Also, size is important. If you have 20 people in your 'team' it is not really a team! You will have sub groups and sub teams within that number. They can all be pointing to the same set of goals but they are not one team.

On the next page is a brief self-assessment you can use to ask yourself and your team some key questions. There are many published questionnaires that measure this sort of thing. It is worth completing some of these as they really open up discussion within teams. For managers, if they are done anonymously, they can give you very rich data. For the consultant looking into a team, they will help you to understand what is going on.

One great resource is a book called, *First, Break All the Rules* by Marcus Buckingham and Curt Coffman of the Gallup Foundation. Another is *Gower's Compendium of Questionnaires and Inventories* by Sarah Cook.

TEAM SELF-ASSESSMENT

Area	Description	Yes or no
Goals	We have clear goals linked to our company's objectives and we all know what they are.	
Roles	People know their roles and have all they need to do their jobs (eg skills, knowledge, equipment).	
Decisions	We have an agreed method for making decisions and everyone contributes to this.	
Management style	The manager is able to adjust his/her style to get the best from the team.	
Disagreement	It is okay to disagree with each other and we resolve our issues in an adult and assertive manner.	
Atmosphere	We interact well and help each other when things get tough.	
Development	Development is encouraged in the team, eg we talk both before and after team members go on courses.	
Feedback	Feedback is welcomed, both upwards, downwards and sideways.	
Talent	We are encouraged to work as much as we can in the areas we are good at.	

STYLE

There is no one best style to use with teams. There is, however, the right style for the stage that the team is at. There has been some great work done on this; see in particular Blanchard's Situational Leadership Model, which can be found in his *One Minute Series*.

Throughout this pocketbook, I will give you some idea of the appropriate style to use to suit the delivery of the activity. The style that is suggested for each stage will be taken from the selection below.

WHICH STYLE WHEN?

OVERVIEW FOR MANAGERS

Style	Description
Tell 'This is what you must do.'	A way of giving information, applicable for short briefings where time is limited. Doesn't allow those on the receiving end to think for themselves so, if over-used, can result in 'passengers' in your team time.
Sell 'This will be really good.'	Similar to the Tell style but with an enthusiastic, motivational feel. You talk about what needs doing and spell out the benefits to the team.
Buy-in 'Look what you will get out of this.'	Overlaps with the Sell style but requires more thought and discussion about what is in it for the team. You tailor what you say based on the responses you receive.
Consult 'What is it that you want or need?'	The consultative manager asks, 'What is it that you want or need from me or the organisation?' A much more hands-off style: you are working to meet the group's needs rather than telling them what they need.
Coach/facilitate	The coaching/facilitating manager aims to pull the answers out from his/her team. The team largely sets the agenda and does a lot of the talking: the manager facilitates the discussion. The manager's role is to shape the output or give support as required, eg 1-1 budget training. You try to be neutral about the output.

WHICH STYLE WHEN?

OVERVIEW FOR TRAINERS

Style	Description
Tell	You are the expert. You listen long enough to get a sense of the problem or situation and then give your 'expert' answer. Team members' involvement is simply to accept or dismiss your idea.
Sell	You use your enthusiasm and charisma to 'jolly' them along. You want them to be excited about what you have to offer. You might use this style at the start of an event to help them engage with you.
Buy-in	In training, this means listening to what participants say and playing it back to 'hook them in'. If someone says, 'I have done this job for years and I've seen this before', you might say later, '…and with all the experience here, in particular Ben who spoke earlier, we know we will get it right'.
Consult	For trainers this means looking for the true causes of problems. If time management is poor in the team, it would be easy just to arrange some training. The consultant trainer probes to find out if the problem is consistent or intermittent. Does everyone have the same issue? Is it a process problem, or IT related, etc.
Coach/ facilitate	This style is about really listening and questioning. You aim to talk as little as possible and mainly pull the answers out from the group. You can afford to be completely neutral as you have no particular answer in mind.

THE LOCUS OF CONTROL

This box is shown four times in the pocketbook during the PAUL model. It is used to illustrate *who has the power*.

For manager, please read team leader or training consultant. Employee can either be team member or training delegate. The next page gives further detail.

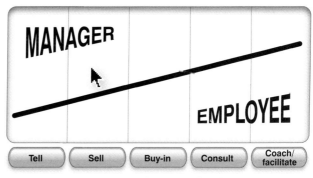

| Tell | Sell | Buy-in | Consult | Coach/facilitate |

(Adapted from Tannenbaum and Schmidt, Pfeiffer's Theories and Models)

THE LOCUS OF CONTROL

The model works from left to right. The further to the left the communication style appears, the more the manager/consultant is doing: the further to the right, the more active the team member is.

The aim of most management models and indeed a lot of training models, is for the team members/delegates to actively engage in what is going on. You want them to take part, to initiate, to question and challenge, and to take responsibility for the process. During team time, this might mean team members taking it in turns to chair the meeting, set the agenda items, share leadership on different things and voluntarily take on tasks.

During training, this means sessions where the delegates are actively involved and participating. You are interested in their views and opinions on the content, and you are keen to explore how they might make best use of their new learning.

POLITE ACTIVITIES

POLITE ACTIVITIES

OVERVIEW

The **polite** stage in team development is most common when the group is newly formed. It can also occur if there is a new manager and everyone is *on their best behaviour*. At this stage people in the team feel awkward and want clarity. They need to know where they stand.

The very basic human ritual of a greeting is essential here. In team terms this means helping people get to know each other. Until this happens people cannot move on to more useful levels of interacting. Imagine a stranger at a party telling you about their latest personal problem when you have only just met. It feels wrong – they have missed out the other necessary stages of acquaintance.

The **polite** activities should be run by the manager or trainer. (The team is too new/immature for members to take this on for themselves.) These activities are about greeting and finding out. Some are quick to run and some are more elaborate.

STYLE

Manager behaviour
This style is the nearest to a directive or telling style. There is high dependence on the manager or leader to provide guidance, action and especially a definite presence.

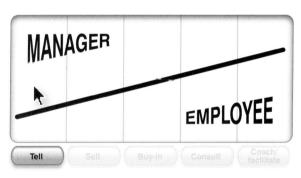

MANAGER

EMPLOYEE

| Tell | Sell | Buy-in | Consult | Coach/facilitate |

Consultant behaviour
The training consultant running these activities needs to be able to use a mixture of styles but should not be surprised when people won't speak up. Prepare to have lots of upbeat, positive banter just in case you are not able to pull all the answers from the team members.

I HAVE A DREAM

Time
20 minutes.

What's the point?
A short activity to get people thinking about how they fit into the 'big picture'.

How

1. Write up the company's mission statement or, even better, vision statement.

2. Ask the group to draw their own dream or vision of where they want to be, personally or at work, in the next 3 years.

3. The pictures should be drawn on to one wall of paper. Then ask the team to discuss the similarities and differences.

4. The next step is for the team to draw this out together in terms of milestones to show that they are on track.

THIS IS WHO I AM

Time
10 minutes (more if you use variations).

What's the point?
To give people a clear and immediate understanding of who you are and what you stand for (or what standards you want to see.)

How

1. Write on flipchart sheets the words **past, present, future**.

2. Underneath each word, write or draw something that is significant and *you want them to know* about you. Under **past**, you might write something like: 'university, Scotland and travelling'.

3. Use your key words or drawings as a springboard to give the team a sense of who you are.

4. Make sure that the information is **brief** and **linked** to the sort of image you want to leave them with (this is a key point).

29

Variations

1. You can use this activity to introduce anything that is important to you, eg standards: *'In the past I have been very involved in Investors in People. This is a theme that has stayed with me and I intend to make sure that in our future you will feel it is as worthwhile as I do.'*

2. Alternatively, ask everyone in the team to present their own 'This is who I am' within a strict time limit of 10 minutes to prepare and 5 minutes to deliver.

3. A further variation is to invite group members to write a team version, highlighting the team's past and present, and identifying what its future might be like.

Note: Variation 3 is good for teams who have already done a lot of meet and greet activities but are still too polite and awkward/formal with each other. It draws out very useful background information to explain why they are stuck at this stage.

MASKING THE FUTURE

Time
5 minutes per person plus 10 minutes preparation.

What's the point?
An active way to help people explain where they have come from and where they are going.

How

1. Stick a long length of masking tape across the floor and write **past** at one end and **future** at the other end.

2. Allow everyone 10 minutes to identify key aspects of their past/present and ambitions for the future.

3. Each person in turn takes a 5 minute walk along the masking tape, from **past** to **future**, giving a verbal overview of their key points.

4. **Top tip** – manager or trainer should go first to model the level of disclosure required.

Variations

1. Hang a washing line across the room instead, to make the activity more visual. At appropriate points along the line participants peg pieces of paper with the key points of their talk. This is a clear way of showing how things are related and in what order.

2. Give out flipchart paper and ask team members to draw stick people to represent their key points. If they work in pairs or threes it will be less 'scary'.

WHAT DO YOU WANT THEN?

Time
10+ minutes (depending on numbers).

What's the point?
A chance to get team leader's and team members' expectations out in the open.

How

1. Give everyone a blank white baseball cap (available from www.thetrainingshop.co.uk) and coloured pens.

2. Allow everyone 5 minutes to draw on the hat their expectations for the team.

3. Everyone then shares what they have drawn or written.

4. Ask questions to encourage individuals to continue talking.

5. **Crucial:** there are no right or wrong answers here; the aim is to find out what people expect or want!

Variations

1. Use T-shirts instead (Primark sells cheap *one size fits all* packs).

2. Get participants to work in small groups and give them blank tablecloths to doodle on.

3. For pairs, use flipchart paper.

Note

Using the gimmick of a hat or T-shirt makes this activity very revealing. Conventional questioning would reveal very little of a group at this stage.

WHEREVER I LAY MY HAT

Timo
10 minutes (longer if you want).

What's the point?
A great way to get people talking. You can use some of the pre-prepared questions overleaf or you can tailor it to whatever you want to know.

How

1. Buy a hat.

2. Print off, cut out and place in the hat a variety of questions (see next page)

3. In turn, ask people to take a question, read it out and give their answer.

4. Continue for as long as you like. You may find that it gets better the longer you keep going as people warm up.

Variations

1. There are countless variations of this activity. If you have specific questions regarding forthcoming change or particular goals, just write the questions to suit.

2. Use a game like Snakes and Ladders. Every time someone lands on a square, they pick a question and answer it. The fun aspect of the game makes it seem much safer to say things people would not normally say.

Questions

Here are 30 examples that you can adapt, type, print off, cut out and put in your hat.

1. What is a nickname you have or have had?

2. How has your life changed from a year ago (besides having children or a new job)?

3. What is your favourite book, and why?

4. What is one of your goals in life?

5. What activity makes you feel alive?

6. In general, do you live for today or plan for tomorrow?

7. If you had a month to do anything you wanted to and cost wasn't a factor, what would you do?

8. Describe one of the best decisions you have ever made?

9. If you had more money what would you change about your life?

10. What is a characteristic in others that you admire?

11. What is a risk you have taken in your life?

12. What is one of your greatest achievements?

13. What is something you do to relax?

14. If heaven exists, what would you want your God to say to you when you arrived there?

15. What is one of the best gifts you have ever received?

16. Who is one of the most interesting individuals you have met and why?

17. Who has had the biggest impact on your life?

18. What was the first job you ever had?

19. What is satisfying about your job?

20. If, like milk and newspapers, you could have anything of your choice delivered to your doorstep every morning, what would you want it to be?

21. Which punctuation mark best describes your personality?

22. If you could swallow a pill that would stop anything of your choice from ever happening to you again, what would the pill permanently end?

23. If people could truly read your mind, what would they discover that you think about most often?

24. If 10 people who know you were asked to choose the one adjective that they feel best describes you, what would be the most common word?

25. If someone were looking for you in a bookstore, in which section would they be most likely to find you?

26. What do you forget to do more than anything else?

27. If you could teach everyone in the world one skill, what would it be?

28. What is your most likeable quality?

29. What is the one thing for years you've been saying you should do but as yet have not done?

30. What is the best piece of advice you've ever received?

(Reproduced with permission of Andy Lothian Junior, Insights International, Dundee)

GUESS WHO?

Time
10 minutes.

What's the point?
A quick way of finding out what people have done in the past, by guessing who said what.

How

1. Ask everyone to write down anonymously, on separate pieces of paper, jobs they have had before, or things they have done, or a hobby they enjoy that they think no one will know about.

2. Fold up the pieces of paper and put them into a hat.

3. Then ask everyone to write, down the left-hand side of a sheet of paper, as many numbers as there are people in the team.

4. When the first slip of paper is pulled from the hat and read out, everyone has to guess who it belongs to and then write that person's name against number 1.

5. When all the slips have been read out, go through the answers and see who got the most right.

6. Spend as little or as long as you like on individual answers, depending on how much you want people to know about each other.

I AM SORRY BUT I HAVE TO DRAW A LINE HERE

Time
10 minutes.

What's the point?
A simple technique to open up discussion about the management styles people want and maybe have experienced in the past.

How

1. On a flipchart or whiteboard, draw a line and along it add wording as shown on the next page.

2. Ask people to put a Post-it® at the point where they would like the manager to be.

3. Ask for practical examples of what that would look or sound like.

4. Tell them, if appropriate, which styles you feel most comfortable using.

5. Ask if there are times when all styles could be appropriate and if so when?

Variation

If they are a quiet group, suggest they work in pairs or threes to help them to talk.

I decide and then tell you | I ask your opinion but I decide | We decide together | You decide but check with me | You decide

POLITE ACTIVITIES

THAT'S YOU THAT IS

Time
10-15 minutes.

What's the point?
To prompt
discussion about
how first
impressions are
not necessarily
accurate but can
be useful anyway.

How

1. Give paper and envelopes to everyone.

2. Ask them to write down their first impression of someone who is in the room with them today.

3. Ask them to think about what that person's previous job might have been, what sort of house they live in, what sort of car they drive, their ambitions or passions, etc.

4. Ask them to seal their thoughts inside the envelope and put the person's name on it.

5. Collect the envelopes and give them out later when it suits you (rule of thumb: do this once people know each other well enough not to get offended).

6. Draw out the point. For example, how do these first impressions relate to how our customers or other internal departments see us? Are we happy with our first impressions?

Variations

1. More challenging version: collect in envelopes as before. Read out the first impression details but don't reveal the name. See how many people guess the person from the description. **Note:** Allow the person who has been described to comment on the first impression, as they may feel the need to justify their behaviour if they are not happy with what they hear.

2. Write impressions of other teams or departments rather than individuals and get everyone to compare their answers.

POLITE ACTIVITIES

RULES OF ENGAGEMENT

Time
10 15 minutes.

What's the point?
To get the essential part of the greeting ritual started correctly by asking people how they actually want to work together, so that you can set up a 'contract' between them.

How

1. Ask people to consider how they want to work together as a group.

2. Divide them into small groups (2-3 people); give each group a plain white T-shirt.

3. Hand out coloured pens and give the groups 6 minutes to decorate their T-shirts with pictures, words and symbols that answer the questions, 'What do we want from each other?' and, 'What are we willing to offer to the group?'.

4. Review each T-shirt allowing approximately 2 minutes per shirt.

5. Ask the following sorts of questions:
   - What do we need to do practically to meet these criteria?
   - What are the common themes in all the T-shirts?
   - Does everyone agree with what we are asking?
   - How will we check that we are doing what we say?
6. Display the T-shirts in the office as a constant reminder.

Variations

1. Use standard flipchart paper instead of T-shirts.

2. Go round the group and ask everyone in turn:
   'What in your opinion is the most important thing we should adhere to?'. Display the answers and indicate clearly who gave them.

WHAT WOULD SUCCESS LOOK LIKE?

Time
15 minutes.

What's the point?
A selection of questions that you can use whenever you need to solve problems as a group, the aim being to make your meetings more productive.

How

1. Display the body coaching model (see next page) on a wall where it is clearly visible.

2. Use the questions as a checklist to make sure you are covering the essential problem-solving questions.

Head questions

Where are we heading?

What will success look like for us?

If we resolved this problem, what would we be saying to ourselves?

What do we think about this problem?

Body questions

What is going on now?

What has been tried already?

How did that work?

How do we feel about it?

What is our gut instinct?

Leg questions

Where could we go for answers/assistance?

What else could we do?

What support do we need?

Feet questions

What are our next steps?

What are the steps after that?

On a scale of 1-10, how committed are we to taking these steps?

Extracts from Body Coaching Model by Paul Tizzard, published in Fenman Coach the Coach Series

NICE WEATHER WE'RE HAVING

CLIMATE CHECKER

Time
2 minutes.

What's the point?
A really quick way to find out how people feel about a particular issue. This can be used at any time during a team's life (see variations).

How

1. On a flipchart or a whiteboard draw a line with a scale of 1-10 on it.

2. Put above the line the statement that you want a vote on or an answer to, eg 'I think that we are excellent at customer service' (10 = strongly agree; 1 = strongly disagree).

3. Ask people to put a mark on the line at the point that represents their answer.

4. Ask questions like:
   - What are the themes here?
   - What might be behind some of the higher scores?
   - What might be behind some of the lower scores?

5. Move on to the next item.

Variations

1. You can edit the question and use it for any situation and at any point. Eg, use it at the beginning of a meeting, halfway through and again at the end to see if people's votes move.

2. At the end of the meeting convert it into a 'scale of agreement'.

Love it

Okay...

Not sure

Live with it

Hate it

ANGRY ACTIVITIES

ANGRY ACTIVITIES

OVERVIEW

When a team is at this stage, there can be large displays of emotion in the negative form of anger, sarcasm and jealousy. You may also meet impatience from people who genuinely want to get on with the job without the interference of 'human dynamics'.

A team can experience such emotion for many reasons but it is generally indicative of change within the team itself, even something as simple as a new member joining.

The activities that follow are intended to be run by training consultants and managers. The main aim of these activities is clarity of purpose and bringing to the surface the things that are really going on but are not said.

STYLE

Manager behaviour

You can expect discomfort at this point as the team start to work out who they are and where they fit in. You need to hold fast to your goals and sense of purpose. Expect to be 'tested' and prepare for how you will deal with it. You may see people challenging each other openly or behind the scenes, and forming cliques. This is not a time to be a shrinking violet. The best approach is to up your levels of enthusiasm, and to help people realise that there is a great team lurking within the disagreement.

Consultant behaviour

Your style should still be facilitative: do not get drawn into the team's politics. It is easy to get caught up in a spiral of negativity here. Stay upbeat, positive and focused.

ANGRY ACTIVITIES

TIMELINE

Time
15 minutes.

What's the point?
A quick method to look at where you are and where you can be. People can often feel quite lost at this stage and need pointing in the right direction.

How

1. Stretch a long piece of masking tape the length of a meeting room wall.

2. At one end of the tape stick a starting date (if possible the date that you started as a team).

3. Plot along the line what has happened to date.

4. Then plot where things are going in the future.

5. Ask people to review progress to date and say how they feel about future plans.

EXPRESS YOURSELF!

Time
10 minutes.

What's the point?
A light-hearted way for people to express their feelings using play dough.

How

1. Give everybody a lump of play dough.

2. Ask them to shape it into how they feel right now or how they see the current situation.

3. Review the bizarre shapes that people produce.

4. Ask questions like, *'What does this lump of play dough mean to you?'*

Note: Some people will find it difficult to talk about their feelings but this is a safe way of getting their thoughts out into the open. I have seen people simply squash the play dough and, when asked to comment, say, *'I feel flat.'*

MIND THE GAP

Time
15 minutes.

What's the point?
Teams identify their own gaps by asking each other a few skilful questions.

How

1. Split the team or group into smaller numbers (threes being the ideal).

2. Ask them to produce an outcome statement for 24 months (or other period) from now, using outcome terminology, eg: 'We are a successful team, we are meeting our targets, we get on well together', etc. (In other words, expressed as if it is already happening.)

3. Ask them to present on a flipchart to the rest of group.

4. Ask them to rate on a scale of 1-10 where they are in relation to the statement that they have just made (10 = nearly there; 1 = nowhere near).

5. Ask them any of the following questions:
   • What is the gap between the two?
   • What would need to happen to close the gap?
   • What small thing could we do every day to get nearer to our goal?
   • What would we need to do to go from a 5 to a 6? (This question could be used with any starting number to simply move one level up.)

6. Make a note of the comments that come out of this session and find out how to put them into practice.

WHAT YOU'RE REALLY GOOD AT

Time
20+ minutes.

What's the point?
An easy to deliver method to get people to give feedback to each other.

How

1. Buy some feedback cards from www.thetrainingshop.co.uk

2. Place all the cards on a table.

3. Ask people to pick up a maximum of 2 cards from the positive pack that they would like to give to others.

4. Ask everyone to explain why they have given certain cards to certain people.

5. Now do the same with cards from the negative pack and ask them to pick one card that they would like to give to someone else. Ask them to explain why.

6. Go round the room and ask people what one thing they were pleased or surprised about.

Feedback rules

- Avoid fluffy statements like, *'You seem really nice...'* This could be made more concrete by saying, *'You seem really nice **because** you always say hello to me every morning...'*

- Take time over the feedback; people can't savour it or think about it if it is delivered too quickly.

- Look the person in the eye when giving the feedback and say things like, *'**You** are good at this because...'*

- When receiving the feedback just listen to it first. Then ask for clarification if it doesn't make sense to you – you don't have to justify any behaviour, just listen to what is said.

Variation

Rather than using cards, put everyone's name in a hat. Everyone picks out a name at random. They then have to give feedback to that person – one thing that is great and one thing that hinders them. Don't be too concerned if they only make positive comments, as this could be to do with the team's current stage of development.

ANGRY ACTIVITIES

WHAT'S YOUR SPORT?

Time
10 minutes.

What's the point?
People in companies work in different types of teams. This short activity uses sport as a metaphor to generate discussion.

How

1. Split the team into pairs or threes.

2. Ask each group to consider what sort of team they think they are. Are they, for example, a cricket team with most people in specialist roles, often playing alone and occasionally coming together as a team? Or are they like a netball or a basketball team where they are constantly moving, reacting quickly to each other's creativity and the actions of the other team?

3. Once they have had a chance to decide what sort of team they are, ask them to spend no more than 1 minute per group telling everyone else their conclusions.

4. Your job is just to listen and ask questions like:

   'What are the similarities and differences between the choices?

   What does this mean to us as a team?

   Are we operating as the right sort of team in light of the challenges we face?'

5. Summarise the whole discussion.

Credit to Andy Cross

ANGRY ACTIVITIES

THE BEST WE CAN BE

Time
10-15 minutes.

What's the point?
Straight individual brainstorm to get people thinking about *the best we can be*. It is positive and aspirational and can help to pull groups up from a low ebb.

How

1. Ask everyone individually to answer the question, *'If this team was the best it could be, what would it look like?'*

2. Ask each one in turn to shout out what they have written and a volunteer to write it all up on the flipchart.

3. Ask the following questions and keep a note of the answers:
   - Which bits of these ideas are we already doing, albeit in a small way?
   - What could we be doing more or less of?
   - What could we be doing differently?
   - What are the next steps?
   - Who will take responsibility for ensuring we take those steps?

ANGRY ACTIVITIES

YOU ARE FLIPPING GREAT!

Time
20 minutes (or less depending on numbers).

What's the point?
An active way for people to give each other feedback.

How

1. Everyone takes a sheet of flipchart paper and names it clearly at the top.
2. Put all the sheets up on the meeting room walls.
3. Everyone then moves around the room and writes feedback on the sheets – one good thing and one thing that the person concerned could do better. (Give a strict time limit so people don't spend forever doing it!)
4. Allow everyone time to read the feedback.
5. Ask each person to give a fair summary of what has come out of this exercise.
6. If brave and time permits, ask individuals if they are going to do anything in the light of the feedback.

Variation

On their own named flipchart paper, ask each individual to write down the things they think they are good at and the things they believe they could improve upon. Everyone then moves around the room with a pen. They are allowed 4 ticks per person to put beside the points they think are the most important (2 ticks for *positives* and 2 ticks for *could do better*). This will give the person feedback only in the areas they themselves have put forward – less risky, therefore.

Top tips

- Focus on goals and outcomes
- Seek compromise and areas of agreement
- Don't be afraid to 'sell' the picture of how things can be different from now
- Listen and let them know it is normal for groups to go through a 'groan zone'
- You can use the climate checker activity (see previous chapter) again here

UNDERSTANDING ACTIVITIES

OVERVIEW

You will begin to see:

- People starting to understand each other better
- More commitment and unity to the purpose
- Fewer cliques
- More respect for the leader/manager
- Humour being used in a more pleasant, non-sarcastic way
- People having a sense of what their roles are

If not managed carefully, there can be a danger of reaching a stalemate or plateau here (some teams can stay at this stage for ever, or so it seems). The main thrust of the activities in this section is to encourage the group not to lose momentum, but to move on. The activities help people to focus on the team's goals. These activities can be run by manager or consultant alike and it is well worth encouraging participants to help in whatever way they can.

STYLE

Manager behaviour

At this stage, the behaviour of the manager is facilitative (see page 105 for some top tips). He/she should be listening and helping the team to make decisions together on team matters. The manager should by now be able 'let go of the reins' a little and spend more time encouraging than chasing.

Consultant behaviour

The consultant should be encouraging everyone to have a voice and making it clear that everyone's right to speak should be respected.

HOW'S IT GOING THEN?

Time
10 minutes.

What's the point?
A simple team discussion approach to introduce the concept that the team needs less involvement from you. You need to be open to ideas and use your facilitation skills by withholding judgement slightly longer than you might normally. For tips on facilitation, see page 105.

How

1. Write on a sheet of flipchart paper the following heading: 'Things are going well in this team – discuss'.

2. Say to the team something like, *'I am really keen to hear everyone's view on this topic. We are going to talk for 10 -15 minutes and someone will take notes* (ask for volunteer at this point). *I am going to hold back my opinion as I want to hear what others have to say. Who would like to start?'* Stay silent until someone speaks!

3. Once the first speaker has finished, encourage others to talk and make sure that everyone gets a chance to contribute.

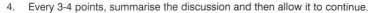

4. Every 3-4 points, summarise the discussion and then allow it to continue.

5. If the conversation dries up, have a couple of questions in reserve,
eg *'What do we do well?'* and, *'What could we be doing more (or less) of?'*.
In a nutshell, you are trying to draw the answers from them, to encourage
them to think and ultimately to self-manage.

Variation

If you are uncomfortable with such a hands-off approach, try the following variation.

Take 3 sheets of flipchart paper:
On sheet 1 write, 'We are a great team because…'
On sheet 2 write, 'We do the following things well…'
On sheet 3 write, 'We could do better in the following areas…'

Split your team into 3 small groups and give each of them one of the sheets. Allow them
10 minutes to discuss and write down their thoughts. Then ask them to present their
comments to the rest of the team. Encourage discussion. Finally, thank them for their
contributions and, between you, agree some possible next steps.

BALLOONS R US

Time
10 minutes.

What's the point?
Use balloons to raise awareness of team emphasis.

How

1. Give everyone in the team 3 balloons.

2. Ask them to consider where the emphasis is in this team in terms of **team**, **task** and **individual** (see next page).

3. Ask them to inflate the balloons to represent the differences in emphasis.

4. Go round the room and ask them why they have inflated the balloons to the size they have.

5. Encourage individuals to speak their minds and stress that it is okay to do this. You are trying to foster autonomy.

Note

John Adair concluded that a team should place equal emphasis on the three areas of *team*, *task* and *individual*. An over-emphasis on one area, will, if it continues for too long, have a detrimental effect on the other areas.

- **Task;** focus on the job and what needs to be done.
- **Team:** focus on creating a sense of team, eg briefings, awaydays, meetings, team goals.
- **Individual:** focus on me, what I want, what I need, my individual goals, 1-1 sessions.

Variation

Ask team to draw circles on a sheet of paper instead of inflating balloons.

UNDERSTANDING ACTIVITIES

SNAKES AND LADDERS

Time
20-30 minutes
(slightly more
complicated to set
up but can be
used repeatedly).

What's the point?
A great way of
getting issues
out in the open
while playing a
game that is
familiar to all.

How

1. Buy Snakes and Ladders or similar game.

2. Think of several issues and ideas that you would like to discuss with the team.

3. Write them on slips of numbered paper (the same number as there are squares on the Snakes and Ladders board).

4. Put numbers on every square (if the board is not already numbered).

5. Each person takes it in turn to roll the dice and move their counter accordingly.

6. When they land on a square, they look at the number on the board, read what it says on the corresponding slip of paper and answer the question.

Examples:

Square 1: Things that I think this team are great at…

Square 2: Things that I think this team could be better at…

Square 3: Two ideas I have to make it more fun in our team…

Square 4: I think that the change that is coming up in our team is…

Square 5: I think that one of this team's blind spots is…

Write down the things you want to discuss. These can be as light-hearted or as serious as you want. The game approach allows people to talk about important things without it seeming threatening.

MEETINGS, MEETINGS, MEETINGS

Time
10+ minutes.

What's the point?
People in teams spend a lot of time in meetings, particularly team meetings. This session is about agreeing some ground rules.

How

1. Remind everyone of existing ground rules (set up during the **polite** stage).

2. Divide the team into small groups.

3. Write the following on a flipchart and give the groups 5 minutes to consider:
   - Meetings go really well when we…
   - Meetings don't go so well when we…

4. Ask them to present their thoughts.

5. Use facilitation skills to gather all the input and compile it into one list that can be used as a checklist for all future meetings.

6. Ask someone to volunteer to be 'team police' to ensure the new rules are followed.

NOMINAL GROUP TECHNIQUE

Time
30+ minutes.

What's the point?
Gets people sharing their ideas, prioritising and problem-solving without the manager or trainer getting involved.

How

1. Give 3 Post-its® to each person in the team and ask them to write down up to 3 issues or problems that they would like to focus on or discuss.

2. Ask them to do this in silence, to write clearly in large letters and have 1 topic per Post-it®.

3. Tell them the information will be confidential and they can write what they like. (NB confidentiality only really works with a large team as small teams will probably recognise each other's writing!)

4. When they have completed their Post-its®, ask them to come and stick them up randomly on the wall or flipchart, or you could collect them in.

5. Now ask someone to cluster the Post-its® into obvious groups.

6. Once you have 4 or 5 clusters, look at the one with the most Post-its® – this is the first area to discuss. Give these Post-its® to one mini group within the team.

7. Give the next largest batch of Post-its® to another mini group.

8. Ask both groups to spend 10 minutes looking at the Post-its® and to come up with some short- and long-term solutions.

9. After 10 minutes or so, ask them to tell the rest of the team their ideas.

10. Write up the suggestions, agree a deadline for action and ask for volunteers to ensure it happens.

Variation

For more ideas, attend the training offered either by **www.pinpoint.uk.com** or **www.thetrainingshop.co.uk**

UNDERSTANDING ACTIVITIES

TALK TALK

Time
10 minutes.

What's the point?
To review the team's communication methods and agree the best medium.

How

1. Divide the team into 3 groups.
2. Write up the following questions and give out one per group:
   - The way we use team briefings is great – discuss
   - The way we use email is great – discuss
   - The way we use the telephone is great – discuss
3. Give them 5 minutes to discuss their topic.
4. Collect in the thoughts.
5. Display the top tips or actions that emerge.

Variation

Join 3 or more pieces of flipchart paper together. Working across the 3 sheets, draw a chart of all the different types of communication that come into the team from other departments, companies or customers and similarly what goes out from the team. Once people have drawn in all the links, ask them to stand back and make comments on what they can see. For example, they may notice lots of arrows coming in to the department from customers but only a few leaving the team (reactive responses).

The trick with this style of working is to make it as large and as visual as possible so that people can see the whole picture and gaps appear more obvious.

GO WITH THE FLOW

Time
15 minutes.

What's the point?
To help groups examine how they communicate with each other and which way the communication flows.

How

1. Draw symbols, evenly spaced apart, to represent each person in the team.

2. Now draw lines from one symbol to another to represent the communication flow.

3. Use different lines/colours for different types of communication eg email, phone, face-to-face.

4. Show the direction of communication flow for each line.

5. Encourage everyone to draw this together.

6. Stand back and ask questions like:

   • What patterns emerge?

   • What direction does the communication seem to move in?

   • Are there any areas of concern?

   • Are there any areas that could be better?

   • Are we using one type of communication too much or not enough?

7. Sum up the comments.

WHAT ARE YOU WORTH?

Time
10 minutes.

What's the point?
When things start to plateau, you need to check that you are on track. This quick exercise will help you think about what value you are adding.

How

1. Pin up the team's objectives or vision statements on the wall bold and clear to read. (If you don't have team plans, use the company objectives.)

2. Draw a line underneath each objective or vision with a scale of 1-10 on it.

3. Ask everyone to put a mark on each scale to answer the question, *'To what extent are we working towards these team or organisation goals?'* (0 = not at all and 10 = fully working towards).

4. After people have voted, ask each one to finish this sentence, *'The way in which I add value by being here is…'*

5. Close the session by asking, *'Is there anything else we can do?'*

UNDERSTANDING ACTIVITIES

SPECTACLES OR MONOCLES?

Time
15 minutes.

What's the point?
To examine whether team members are playing to their strengths and whether their current jobs suit them.

How

1. Give out paper and ask everyone to draw a circle and write 'work' in the middle.

2. Now ask them to draw another circle which represents how they see themselves relative to their job roles (see examples overleaf).

3. The aim is a balanced overlap which allows a person to do most of what they like doing, with some stretch to keep their interests up.

4. Ask individuals to discuss what they have drawn and whether there are ways that they could move closer to their ideal way of working. For example, if someone likes to be creative and off the wall, does the job allow for that?

Note

This cannot be exact but gives an indication of how people see the way they work and how it fits with their **preferred** way of working. Eg, if I like detail and accuracy, I would hope that my job allows me the scope and time to work to this standard. If my actual job is always chopping and changing and does not allow me to meet my standards, I will not be working within my preferences and may not, eventually, enjoy the job.

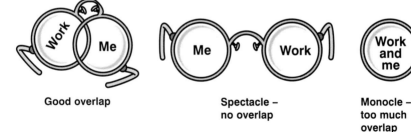

Good overlap

Spectacle –
no overlap

Monocle –
too much
overlap

LEARNING ACTIVITIES

LEARNING ACTIVITIES

OVERVIEW

At this stage you will see people learning from what they do and being more open with each other about strengths and weaknesses. Encourage them to play to their strengths.

- People open to feedback
- Sharing ideas more readily
- Higher levels of trust
- Coping with disagreement and even welcoming differences of opinion
- More autonomous and checking with you less
- Looking out for each other and volunteering help

STYLE

Manager behaviour

By now you should be more hands-off; mainly overseeing and delegating. Assuming a good relationship with your team, you can use a mixture of leadership styles according to individual needs. Use questions to help people solve their own problems. Emphasize that it is the end result that matters not the way that it is reached. Encourage people to work with each other, help each other to learn and make the most of on-the-job learning.

Consultant behaviour

The aim now is to help the group solve their own issues. They will probably even want to set their own agenda. Help them to discuss how to make the best of their mix of talents and how to share responsibility with the manager for decision-making across the team.

IT'S ALL IN YOUR HEAD

Time
20+ minutes.

What's the point?
Using Edward De Bono's *Six Thinking Hats*, the group examine the way they approach problem solving and will recognise the style that they use most often.

How

1. Introduce the basic model (see diagram).

2. Ask them, as a group, to identify whether they tend to use one type of thinking more than another.

3. Then ask them to identify individually the one or two hats that they tend to prefer using and how they feel about that.

4. Once they have considered their own processes and their individual preferences, ask them to address the following:
   - Which hat would they like to visit more often in future meetings?
   - If they had to agree the order in which they would like to try the hats, what would it be? Eg first white, then red, then green, etc.

5. Bring to a close and write up the conclusions from the session and what they have learned.

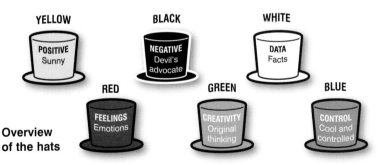

Overview of the hats

YELLOW — POSITIVE Sunny

BLACK — NEGATIVE Devil's advocate

WHITE — DATA Facts

RED — FEELINGS Emotions

GREEN — CREATIVITY Original thinking

BLUE — CONTROL Cool and controlled

Variation

Buy some coloured hats from www.thetrainingshop.co.uk and ask team members to put them on when they want to make a certain point during the meeting. For instance, they could put the red hat on when they want to air feelings.

Overview of the hats

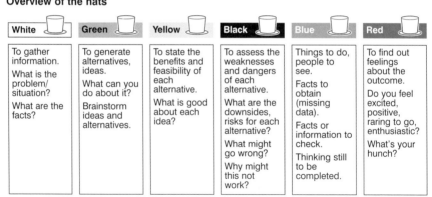

White	Green	Yellow	Black	Blue	Red
To gather information.	To generate alternatives, ideas.	To state the benefits and feasibility of each alternative.	To assess the weaknesses and dangers of each alternative.	Things to do, people to see.	To find out feelings about the outcome.
What is the problem/ situation?	What can you do about it?	What is good about each idea?	What are the downsides, risks for each alternative?	Facts to obtain (missing data).	Do you feel excited, positive, raring to go, enthusiastic?
What are the facts?	Brainstorm ideas and alternatives.		What might go wrong?	Facts or information to check.	What's your hunch?
			Why might this not work?	Thinking still to be completed.	

Ref: *Six Thinking Hats*, Edward De Bono (Penguin Books)

WHAT WERE YOU THINKING?

Time
15 minutes.

What's the point?
An open session where team members can examine what their thinking process has been and how they have been misleading themselves!

How

1. Introduce the concept of rational emotive behaviour therapy. (In a nutshell, it is not what happens to you but your attitude to what happens to you. For example, 2 people can be made redundant from the same office: one will see it as an opportunity while the other will feel hard done by. The same event but a different thought pattern.)

2. The theory continues that if you think something, your actions will follow suit.

3. Ask the team to consider the following questions and facilitate the answers in a review:

- Have we, as a team, ever convinced ourselves of something that later turned out to be completely wrong?
- Is there anything going on now about which we are holding on to certain beliefs?
- If yes, what has been the impact?
- What different thoughts should we be having?

Note: This is subtle but very important. If I believe, for example, that a change the company is going through is wrong and unfair, my actions will follow suit. If I decide to change my mind and think, *'Let's see how it goes and I will give it my best'*, I will act differently as a result.

LEARNING ACTIVITIES

A SOLUTIONS FOCUS

Time
20+ minutes.

What's the point?
A powerful, positive but short session to reflect on what the team already does well and how to do more of it.

How

1. Split the team into small groups and give them any of the following questions to consider for 10 or so minutes. You don't need to give out all the questions; often just 1 or 2 of those on the next page are enough to make the point.

2. Once they have shared their stories in a small group, ask them to do the same with the whole team.

3. Your job is to ask lots of questions and encourage the individuals to share more of the story or experience.

4. This session should feel very positive, so you could ask one of the group to sum up how it has been.

Questions for the group to consider:

1. What is working fine and doesn't need any change?

2. What ideas or advice would a consultant put forward when looking at our issues?

3. It is 12 months from now and everything in the company is great. What needs to have happened over that year to make it come true?

4. Imagine yourselves as customers of your team or company: in 1 year from now, what are you saying about the company?

5. Imagine a magic wand has been waved and from tomorrow everything has been put right. What is the first thing you notice? What are all the other tiny things you notice that are different? In what way are some of these things already happening or have happened in the past, and what do we need to do to get more of it?

Not everyone feels comfortable running this sort of session, as most companies tend to take a problem-orientated approach to fixing what is wrong. Eg, a typical response by a trainer when reading delegate feedback is: *'I know 9 people loved the course, but why did 1 person hate it?! I had better ask him/her what I need to change?'* A solutions focus looks at what is good: how to do more of what is working? Why not ask the 9 people what else you could do to make it even better?

10 great solutions questions that you can use in any of your meetings

1. What would need to happen today to make this meeting worth your while?
2. On a scale of 1-10, how well is this team functioning?
3. What has been better since we last met?
4. What would each team member like the others to know about them and how would that knowledge be significant to the team?
5. What will you be doing differently after today?
6. What will you see more of as these problems dissolve?
7. What has this problem kept us from succeeding in?
8. Tell me about a previous time when you have successfully dealt with a problem like this?
9. Where would we like to be before we meet again?
10. What small things will be happening in the future that will tell us all that things are getting better?

LEARNING ACTIVITIES

A PROPER BRAINSTORM

Time
15 minutes.

What's the point?
To highlight the rules of a brainstorm (in case you have never run one) and to show the benefits of many minds looking at a problem. At this stage of team development brainstorm sessions should be very useful.

How

1. Get plenty of flipchart paper and pens ready.

2. Set the scene, saying, *'I am going to collect all your ideas. There are no rights or wrongs because we can evaluate later. I am keen to hear from anyone and everyone, the sillier the better'.*

3. Put the title of the session at the top of the page, eg '50 ways to use a paper cup...'

4. Start writing. **Most important rule** – write their words exactly as they say them! Interpreting is subtle judgement and will kill the process.

5. If their idea is too long to write down quickly enough, ask **them** to summarise it for you. Then say, *'Does this capture what you were saying?'*

6. Only after the last person has completely finished do you say, *'Right, which of these ideas have merit?'*

7. Be careful not to rubbish any ideas, no matter how daft they may seem.

8. If you are running this brainstorm, then you have no opinion – it is the only way it can work.

Variation

Instead of you writing, give people unlimited Post-it® pads. Then ask them to write one idea per Post-it® and to stick the ideas up on a board as they write them.

LEARNING ACTIVITIES

FERGIE & ANDREW

Time
15 minutes.

What's the point?
Using metaphor to get people having fun and thinking creatively.

How

1. Introduce the exercise as a brainstorm warm-up and fun activity.

2. Think of a metaphor that captures the essence of what you want to get people thinking about (see example on the next page).

3. Then ask people to **apply** the answers to the actual situation.

Situation

Two teams have to merge. They used to be one team many years ago and were then split up. The new merger needs to go well and you want to approach it in an innovative way.

'Today, folks, it is our job to help the reunion of Fergie and Andrew. This is a just a bit of fun and a warm-up before we do the proper brainstorm. As you know, they split up many years ago but there is talk of them getting back together. We have to make sure it goes as well as possible. What do we need to consider?'

Write everything they say, no matter how daft (in fact the sillier the better) on the left-hand side of a sheet of flipchart paper. Encourage the silly contributions especially. When they have run out of ideas, say something like, *'Okay, it was a bit of a trick because this session is actually about your situation of merging. So, how can we directly translate your ideas here into our situation now?'*

You literally draw the parallel across, point for point, until you end up with two lists on the flipchart. The left-hand side shows the Fergie/Andrew situation. The right-hand side is now a list of possibilities for your situation.

This works a storm if you take the risk that people will be able to make the links. They always do.

Top tip

Find a metaphor that people can **really** relate to in your groups and set it up as a practice session before the 'real stuff' begins!

Fergie and Andrew	Our two teams merging again
· Champagne	· Social event
· Marriage guidance	· Take advice - HR???
· Romantic atmosphere	· Right setting - somewhere neutral
· Learn about each other	· Icebreakers
· Someone make first move	· Good leadership
· Bridal suite	· Off site?

HELLO LOVEY

Time
15 minutes.

What's the point?
A bit of fun about imagining the future which will work with lively teams.

How

1. Set the challenge of retelling the team's story to date or predicting how the team will be in 2 years' time.

2. Give everyone 5 minutes to plan whether they will write a poem, adapt a song or act out a play. They then have 10 minutes to perform.

3. Have fun, no other real purpose.
   Works well with a team at this stage.

Variation

If the team are really game, buy or hire some cheap costumes and give them out as props. You could have a cheesy award ceremony at the end.

A-Hmm

LEARNING ACTIVITIES

FIRST IMPRESSIONS – LAST IMPRESSIONS

Time
20 minutes.

What's the point?
A fun activity to close down a team or to use for reflection on the stage the team has reached.

How

1. Ask the team to think about one another and be prepared to discuss the following:
   - My first impression of each person here was…
   - My impression now is…
   - What I have learned from each person is…
   - What I would like to thank individuals for is…

2. Ask each person in turn for their comments.

3. Once everyone has finished, ask for any closing thoughts.

Variation

Give them the introduction they deserve. Each individual picks someone at random and gives them a fabulous introduction based on all the positive things they know about them now. Try it as a poster advert on a flipchart and it is even more fun.

MANAGEMENT ESSENTIALS

MANAGEMENT ESSENTIALS

INTRODUCTION

This section contains short activities and discussion points on 3 key skill areas:

- Facilitation skills (running meetings well)
- Presenting yourself and your case
- Coaching fundamentals (getting the best from individuals and encouraging a productive environment in the team)

The sessions can be used as 'learning events' in a team setting, and can be run by the manager/team leader or a trainer working with the team.

SESSION 1: FACILITATION SKILLS

Time
40+ minutes.

What's the point?
For the team to talk about facilitation and decide how they can use it to run meetings better, get the best from one another, solve problems as a group and bring out their creativity.

How

1. Write these statements on a flipchart:
    *   'Facilitation is about helping groups to solve their own problems.'
    *   'A facilitator is a content neutral person who helps the group to solve their own problems themselves.'
    *   'Facilitators use the following skills or belief systems:
        - The group have the ability to solve their own problems
        - The facilitator is neutral and therefore never expresses an opinion
        - It is just as important to focus on the group dynamics as on what is being said.'

2. Split the team into smaller groups and ask them to consider the following questions:
    - What would need to happen to make all our meetings worthwhile?
    - To what extent could we incorporate some of the features of facilitation?
    - If we do this what might the potential challenges be?

3. Allow the groups about 20 minutes for discussion.

4. Feed back in the larger group and allow about 5 minutes max per group.

5. Draw out themes and then ask, *'What elements can we take from this discussion that will aid us as a team in the future?'*

6. Agree when these new actions will start.

Optional extension to facilitation session – 20 minutes

Ask if anyone would like to try facilitating a discussion. They would need to start a debate within the group and practise withholding their opinion during the discussion.

You can use any topic, eg 'The current Prime Minister is great – discuss'. Or, 'Manchester United are the best football team ever – discuss'.

The facilitator is not necessarily looking for an answer to the question, but just practising withholding his or her opinion so that other people can give theirs freely, without being judged.

Review afterwards and make sure that the volunteer gets lots of praise.

Key points for facilitators

This session works best if you role model what facilitation is about.
The critical thing is not to judge what is being said but just allow people to talk freely.
Here are some key points to observe.

1. You are there to be neutral.

2. Listen and observe.

3. Try to separate facts from feelings when people are talking, eg 'That will **never** work!' sounds like a fact but is a feeling.

4. Reflect back what people are saying, *'Let me check my understanding, what you are saying is…'*. Or, *'Let me summarise what I think I heard…'*.

5. Hold a mirror to the group when facilitating and say, *'I have noticed that 3 people are talking but 4 are not, why is that?'*

6. If you feel odd or notice anything different when working with a group, they are probably aware of it as well. It is worth acknowledging it by saying, *'I don't know about you, but I am feeling a little lost – does anyone else feel like that?'*

7. Aim to talk no more than 20% of the time.

8. They have the answers not you. Encourage them to think about things.

9. Suspend your opinions and stop your face reacting when someone says something you disagree with.

10. Always write the topic or objective for the meeting or session somewhere very visible so that everyone can see it at every point of the discussion.

Conclusion to this session

The aim is to help the group members learn with each other about a key skill that can be enormously powerful when present in a group. For more tips, see *The Facilitator's Pocketbook* by John Townsend and Paul Donovan.

MANAGEMENT ESSENTIALS

SESSION 2: PRESENTING YOURSELF & YOUR CASE

Time
30 minutes.

What's the point?
People talk too much in a lot of meetings and briefings. The average attention span is about 10 minutes, so people need to learn to get to the point more quickly.

How

1. Split the group in half.

2. Draw a smiley face at the top of a sheet of flipchart paper. Give one group 10 minutes to think about great presentations or team meetings when they felt awake, alert and interested.

3. On another sheet draw a grumpy face, and ask the other group to spend 10 minutes thinking about awful presentations when they have lost the will to live.

4. Give each group 5 minutes to talk through their lists.

5. Now combine the lists to come up with 10 rules for the team to use for delivering information in all future meetings and presentations.

You need to role model this to give an example of good presentation practice. Here are some ideas:

1. Keep it short and simple.

2. Use plain spoken English not Victorian written English.

3. Open with a 'bang!', or an interesting story to arouse interest.

4. Be yourself.

5. Use some structure (see below).

6. Give the group a task early on so you get a break, *'For 2 minutes I would like you to write a goal for this session...'*. This gives you a chance, should you need it, to regain composure.

7. Repeat your key messages 3-7 times to make them stick.

8. Link your information to things they already know, eg, *'It's a bit like when you...'*.

9. Try something different! (Attention span is about 10 minutes.)

10. Pause often and remember to breathe.

11. Make sweeping eye contact.

12. Slow down!

Presentation Structure

My 2 top tips for presenting information to others are:

1. **Be yourself**. If you aren't funny, don't try to be. Be natural but just project a little more of your personality than normal.

2. **Structure your messages**. When people are listening and trying to make sense of information, they need boxes to put it into. Watch the news; they always use this technique. They tell you what is going to happen, how many stories there are and the main headlines before they actually tell you the stories.

The simple structure here and on the next page can be used for any presentation without advance preparation. You need, in sequence, the ABCD model, BBC (the 3 Tell 'ems) and KISS.

Attention getter In a recent survey, we found that 1 in 5 people…
Benefits to you for listening are…
Credibility Who am I to talk to you? I have been in charge of this project for…
Direction A rough idea of what is coming up for you is…

The **ABCD** gives you your catchy opening.

Beginning   Tell 'em what you are going to tell 'em
Body   Tell 'em
Conclusion   Tell 'em what you told 'em

> The **BBC** gives you an overall structure just like they use on the news.

Keep **I**t **S**hort and **S**imple.
People do not need to know every single detail.
Tell them the highlights and back it up with detailed handouts if need be.
Give their ears a break and keep it punchy!

Conclusion to this session

Some of these ideas may seem obvious, even old news. But in team presentations in companies all over the UK these basic rules are broken and people are slipping into trances. A few simple tweaks to your approach and, instead of dreading your presentations, people will enjoy their brevity and actually remember your key messages.

Credit to Alan Evans

SESSION 3: COACHING

Time
30 minutes.

What's the point?
The 1-1 skill of coaching, done well, is phenomenally powerful. This session helps the group to explore whether they are already using coaching and if they could use it more.

How

1. Take 3 sheets of flipchart paper and on each one write one of the following statements:

   - 'I have enough time to talk about my development to someone significant'
   - 'Our monthly 1-1 meetings are useful to me'
   - 'I contribute equally to anything to do with my development or appraisals'

2. Ask the whole team, individually and in silence, to rate the statements on a scale of 1-10 (10 being high).

3. Give the group 2 minutes to rush up to the flipcharts, write their own score anonymously onto each sheet and then sit down again.

4. Go through each flipchart in turn and ask for general comments on what is going well and what could be better (ask someone to make notes).

5. Agree next steps between you for what needs to change.

Top tips
There are many theories about the nature of coaching. It is useful to have a definition and a general framework, which I have put below. You might want to share the definition with the group before starting this exercise.

Definition
'Coaching is about helping people to learn. It is not just about teaching them.'
W. Timothy Gallwey. *Inner Game of Tennis*.

Framework

1. The main job when coaching is to help the other person to set goals and then help him/her to achieve them.

2. Don't give advice.

3. Use questions that start with: *who, what, where, when, how*.

4. Listen to the end of the sentence before formulating your next question.

5. Your question should follow on from their last answer.

6. Aim to keep questions to 6-8 words.

7. Summarise every 2-3 points to show you are listening.

8. They have the answer in their heads – they just don't know it sometimes.

9. Practise whenever you can to make it more natural.

10. You are not a counsellor – you are interested in the future not the past.

Conclusion to this session

Coaching is a fantastic skill to have. Not everyone will make a great coach but learning a few basic rules will dramatically improve your working relationships. For more tips, please consult *The Coaching Pocketbook* by Ian Fleming.

TEAMBUILDING SCENARIOS

TEAMBUILDING SCENARIOS

NEW MANAGER WITH NEW TEAM
DEALING WITH EXPECTATIONS

This section is designed as a quick reference to dip in to and choose appropriate activities. The scenarios described are typical situations that occur in teams.

New manager with new team: dealing with expectations

This scenario fits neatly within the **polite** section of the PAUL model. It is about the new manager setting competencies and standards of behaviour.

1.   Use appropriate examples of self-disclosure. It can make you seem more human if you disclose something of your personality. Eg, *'I am great at getting projects up and running but not always so good with the detail. If anyone in this team is, we will be able to work really well together.'*

2. Learn about team members before you join them. Listen a lot, interview and chat to individuals. Ask customers and other departments how the team are perceived. Make notes. Share examples of your knowledge early on, so team members get a sense that you know what you are talking about.

3. Use the first example of *bad* behaviour to show what you are made of! People may test you as a manager. Think about those early impressions and when someone crosses a *line* make sure you address it so that you are not considered a push over.

4. Quick intro – **be brief be bright be gone**. When you first meet the team, set out your stall and deliver succinctly. Tell them your plans: keep it positive, upbeat and, most of all, brief.

5. What is our charter of behaviour? Ask them how things are done around here. Ask: *'If there was one thing that you really wanted or didn't want from me, what would it be?'*

6. You are now on stage. Present yourself and your case well. See the **learning** section for tips but a brief true example might help make the point. One CEO I know opened the manager's briefing with a single PowerPoint slide of a toilet. He was new and everyone was expecting an amazing high-tech presentation. He said, *'The picture of the toilet is to represent the fact that we need to discuss something that no one wants to talk about – just like the toilet. This issue is important – we must not avoid it any more.'* He then delivered his one main unsavoury message and sat down. Guess which presentation people remembered after the manager's briefing?!

7. Build a balanced team. Look for the gaps in the team. What sort of people do you not have who would make it a higher performing team? Work it out and then, when you can, start to recruit them.

NEW MANAGER WITH A TIRED TEAM

This is a tricky situation as the team has a history (and even more difficult if you were once one of the tired ones!).

1. Get to know them 1-1. Arrange meetings and really listen.

2. Lay out your stall. Tell them what you are going to do differently (don't expect them to get excited).

3. Use the past/present/future exercise: 'This is who I am' (see page 29).

4. Try picture boarding. Get them, as a group, to draw pictures to show the team's history, where they see it now and what the future will look like. (You must use pictures or it gets too logical.)

5. Consider a 'coaching with teeth' approach where you ask tough coaching questions. Eg, *'I understand that you think you should have been promoted 2 years ago – how much longer will you be saying that?'* *'What **is** in your control to do about this situation?'* *'What have you done about this problem so far?'* More information can be found in *Body Coaching* in the Coach the Coach series released by Fenman.

6. Ask, *'How do you solve problems round here?'* Find out what processes they use. Most teams don't have any agreement around how they make decisions. This could link into the 'What would success look like' activity in the **polite** section on page 47.

7. **Be the change you want to see**. Stay positive, don't bad mouth others and generally role model the behaviours you want from others. Eg, if you would like to see people taking risks and making decisions in your absence, you have to be seen to actively support people when it goes wrong!

8. Encourage well-managed disagreement. Say, *'It is okay to disagree. We can be tough on the problems not the people.'* If you find this difficult, try imagining you have a bubble around you that no one can get into. This prevents you from taking it personally (anyone who has worked in Customer Service will know this technique).

KEEPING A TEAMBUILD ALIVE

1. Whether you are the manager or consultant working with the team, don't run a teambuilding event until you have both agreed measurable objectives that will occur as a result of it.

2. Plan a date to review the output and stick to it!

3. Pin up the output from the team event in the office so it is very clear for all to see.

4. Ensure that the activities planned for your event are easily transferred back to the workplace, eq workplace type projects.

5. Take lots of photos during the event and pin them up afterwards as a visual reminder.

TEAM THAT HAS BEEN THROUGH CHANGE

When a team has had any sort of upheaval, it is natural that feelings of resentment, anger, frustration or even betrayal will be left over. This is entirely normal. It sometimes helps groups to know this. One model that teams always like is the adapted Kubler-Ross curve below. If your group has seen this already, use another model: the point is to make it big and visual.

The change curve

1. Introduce the change curve by drawing the picture opposite.

2. Ask them to put a marker where they think they are.

3. Ask them the following sort of questions:
   - Where have you put yourself?
   - What is going on for you that puts you there?
   - Where would you like to be?
   - What would need to happen to move there?

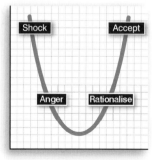

TEAM WITH SPECIFIC ISSUES
HOW DO I DRAW THEM OUT?

You need a process and there are several that work very well if you can stick to the rules of facilitation. Most important is neutrality, which means not contaminating the data by interfering with people's contributions.

Easy 'no preparation' method

1. Give out Post-its® to everyone present.

2. Ask them to write down the team's top three issues.

3. Ask the group to come up in silence and cluster the Post-its® into obvious common groupings.

4. Discuss two clusters that people have written the most about, using facilitation techniques mentioned in the **learning** section.

5. Write up any actions that come out of the discussions.

It is an easy method, but if you are not used to running this sort of thing, you should practise beforehand to get it right. On the day, don't contaminate the data by giving your opinion or judging what anyone has written.

More involved methods for drawing out specific issues

Try the following activities which are contained within this pocketbook:

LAST WORD

Not every group manages to become a high
performing team, or indeed needs to.
It is, however, worth striving for.

Once you have been in
one, it is harder to work
in a shadow of a team
afterwards.

About the Author

Paul Tizzard
When Paul is not running his favourite courses around
coaching, team development, train the trainer or speaking at
seminars, he works as director of Virgin Atlantic's *Flying
Without Fear* programme.

Contact
Paul can be contacted at: paul@flyingwithoutfear.co.uk

Paul Tizzard
P O Box 289
Betchworth
RH3 7LT

Tel: 01737 841095

For a free report on writing your own icebreakers, please go to www.trainersense.com

Customers in USA should contact: Management Pocketbooks, 2427 Bond Street,
University Park, IL 60466. Telephone: 866 620 6944 Facsimile: 708 534 7803
E-Mail:mp.orders@ware-pak.com Web: www.managementpocketbooks.com